Faith Journey

Faith Journey
welcome to the family of God

NAVPRESS

For a free catalog
of NavPress books & Bible studies call
1-800-366-7788 (USA) or 1-800-839-4769 (Canada).

www.NavPress.com

The Navigators is an international Christian organization. Our mission is to advance the gospel of Jesus and His kingdom into the nations through spiritual generations of laborers living and discipling among the lost. We see a vital movement of the gospel, fueled by prevailing prayer, flowing freely through relational networks and out into the nations where workers for the kingdom are next door to everywhere.

NavPress is the publishing ministry of The Navigators. The mission of NavPress is to reach, disciple, and equip people to know Christ and make Him known by publishing life-related materials that are biblically rooted and culturally relevant. Our vision is to stimulate spiritual transformation through every product we publish.

© 2008 Youth for Christ International Ministries
All rights reserved. No part of this publication may be reproduced in any form without written permission from NavPress, P.O. Box 35001, Colorado Springs, CO 80935. www.navpress.com

NAVPRESS and the NAVPRESS logo are registered trademarks of NavPress. Absence of ® in connection with marks of NavPress or other parties does not indicate an absence of registration of those marks.

ISBN-13: 978-1-60006-314-5
ISBN-10: 1-60006-314-4

Cover design by Arvid Wallen
Cover image by Shutterstock

Some of the anecdotal illustrations in this book are true to life and are included with the permission of the persons involved. All other illustrations are composites of real situations, and any resemblance to people living or dead is coincidental.

Unless otherwise identified, all Scripture quotations in this publication are taken from the *Holy Bible, New Living Translation* (NLT), copyright © 1996, 2004. Used by permission of Tyndale House Publishers, Inc., Carol Stream, Illinois 60188. All rights reserved.

Printed in the United States of America

1 2 3 4 5 6 7 8 / 12 11 10 09 08

Contents

Acknowledgments	7
Introduction: Beginning Your Faith Journey	9
SESSION ONE: Entering a Relationship with God	15
SESSION TWO: Who Is God?	21
SESSION THREE: God the Father	29
SESSION FOUR: The Father and You	37
SESSION FIVE: The Son of God	43
SESSION SIX: Jesus as Man and Savior	49
SESSION SEVEN: God the Holy Spirit	57
SESSION EIGHT: The Holy Spirit and Us	63
SESSION NINE: The Father, Son, and Holy Spirit	69
SESSION TEN: Jesus as Lord	75
SESSION ELEVEN: Living Like Jesus	81
SESSION TWELVE: Plan for Daily Growth	91

Bonus!

Becoming a Loving Parent	101
God the Father — A True Story	103
I Am Your Father	105
The Son	107
Understanding Salvation	109

Loving Like Jesus	111
Quiet Time Guide	113
Small Group Leader's Guide	
How to Lead a Small Group	119
Group Discussion Starters	121
Youth for Christ	127

Acknowledgments

We are indebted to the many dedicated men and women of Youth for Christ over numerous years who have worked tirelessly to bring this material to you in its current form. In this regard, we are grateful to the following people:

Lori Hill	Emmanuel Kingi
Joy Englesman	Ken Aringo
Don Osman	Nthenya Masyuko
Dave Bidwell	Lucy Miruka
Emmanuel Chijindu	Beatrice Wangwe
Cyprian Yobera	Felix Mwangi
Seneiya Kamotho	Gowi Odera
Nick Sikobe	T.V.O. Lamptey
Sandy Weiss	Jane Gumo
Banda Banda-di-Mamoso	Jack and Polly Wilson
Ayo Ipinmoye	Chris Harding
George Tabu Jabulani	

We are also indebted to our brothers and sisters from all over Africa who birthed this project and field-tested it as part of the Generation 21 initiative. Through the vision God gave them of empowering young leaders for their continent, this material was developed.

As the worldwide movement of Youth for Christ has adopted this same focus of empowering young leaders, we have modified and adapted this material for worldwide use.

This material is used as a tool to achieve Youth for Christ's strategic focus of reaching young people everywhere, working together with the local church and other like-minded partners to raise up lifelong followers of Jesus who lead by their godliness in lifestyle, devotion to the Word of God and prayer, passion for sharing the love of Christ, and commitment to social involvement.

Beginning Your Faith Journey

The Bible is a wonderful book that contains everything we need to know in order to live our lives the way our Creator intended (see 2 Timothy 3:16-17). In the Bible God shows us how we disobeyed Him and were separated from Him by our sin. Then, through the history, poetry, and wisdom of this book, He shows how we can come back to Him. The Bible is God's Word to us and the main way in which we can hear Him speak. The Bible holds countless truths to live by, but its basic message is God calling us all back to be in relationship with Him.

Our Sin

The reason we are separated from God is sin. Sin is disobedience to God through doing what is wrong or not doing what is right. Romans 3:23 says, "For everyone has sinned; we all fall short of God's glorious standard." This means no one is without sin.

One huge result of our sin is that it separates us from God. He is so holy and perfect that we, with sin in our lives, cannot come close to Him. Isaiah 59:1-2 reminds us of this separation by saying, "Listen! The LORD's arm is not too weak to save you, nor is his ear too deaf to hear you call. It's your sins that have cut you off from God. Because of your sins, he has turned away and will not listen anymore."

Ultimately, our sin results in death. Romans 6:23 says, "For the wages of sin is death, but the free gift of God is eternal life through Christ Jesus our Lord."

Unfortunately, there is nothing we can do on our own to solve this problem.

The Solution

The Bible, however, says that there is a solution. Did you notice the second half of Romans 6:23? The part that says, "The free gift of God is eternal life through Christ Jesus our Lord"? Jesus is the solution! Jesus talks about Himself in John 3:16, saying that God (His Father) loved us so much that He sent Jesus to take the punishment we deserve for our sin, taking our place and dying for us. Jesus, because He loved us, died instead of us so that we could have a relationship with God forever. What amazing love! First John 4:10 says, "This is real love—not that we loved God, but that he loves us and sent his Son as a sacrifice to take away our sins."

By taking the punishment we deserve, Jesus opened the way for us to have a relationship with God that would otherwise be impossible for us.

Now it's up to us to either trust Jesus by asking Him to lead and direct us, or live separately from Him. Being faithful to God is about accepting Jesus Christ's right to rule us, teach us, and show us how to live. We become God's children and give up our rights, trusting only in Christ to make us acceptable to God. John 1:12 tells us of this new privilege we are given by saying, "But to all who believed him and accepted him, he gave the right to become children of God."

Do you want to live a life of service and obedience to Jesus? Or are you, like most of humanity, more concerned about being in charge of your own life? These are tough questions to think through, and you only have a few options:

- Option 1: Follow Jesus; trust His Word, surrender your right to serve yourself, and put your faith and confidence in Him.
- Option 2: Reject Jesus; choose not to believe in God's offer of salvation, trust only in yourself, and deny the guidance and love of Jesus.
- Option 3: Put off any change until a more convenient time. The problem with this is that you risk never finding fulfillment and peace because there may never be a convenient time to make a change.

The answer is often found in realizing that the hunger and longing you have in your heart is actually all about Him. There is a word in the Bible, *shalom,* that means completeness, wholeness, and harmony, a peace and safety.

We all have a hunger in our hearts for this, and it's wonderful to realize that this hunger is really all about Jesus. Isaiah 9:6 describes Jesus as the Prince of Peace, the *Sar Shalom*. Jesus is the only one who can bring completeness, harmony, and peace to our lives.

You don't have to know everything about God now, but you can become committed to finding out and following Him throughout your life. In fact, that's what this book is all about—helping you get to know Jesus personally and follow Him forever.

Your Choice

If you haven't ever thought of becoming a follower of Jesus, there's no better time than right now to do so. This is the point at which your story can change and you can become a new person.

Jesus gives His followers the gift of salvation and forgives all of our sins—every single one! It doesn't matter what we've been doing or what we've done. The gift is open to everyone. You can experience peace with God through Christ.

To become a follower of Jesus Christ right now, you only need to ask Him. Jesus said in Matthew 11:28, "Come to me, all of you who are weary and carry heavy burdens, and I will give you rest." He also said, "Those the Father has given me will come to me, and I will never reject them" (John 6:37).

So if you ask to be His follower and servant, you will be accepted. It's your choice whether to ask or not.

The way followers of Jesus talk to Him is through prayer—which is simply talking and listening. Your prayer should be your own, from your own heart to His. However, if you're not in the habit of talking to God, here's an example of a prayer you can use to begin your relationship with Jesus:

> Our Father in heaven, I know I haven't believed or had faith in you before, but I need your forgiveness and your peace. I now believe that your Son, Jesus, died on a cross to pay the penalty for my sin and came back to life. I am so grateful that, because of this, I can be saved. I want to serve you, Jesus, to join my story with your story forever. So I ask you to come into my life, to direct and take charge of me forever. In Jesus' name I pray, amen.

a new life

The Bible says, "Everyone who calls on the name of the Lord will be saved" (Romans 10:13). So if you have asked Him to be your Lord and Master, and believe He died to save you, you have now begun a lifelong journey with Jesus! Not only will you have peace in Him but you'll also have a new direction, the beginning of a new life story.

Since we live in a world that doesn't follow Jesus, there will be many challenges for you, even persecution and hardships (see 2 Timothy 3:12). Therefore, it's essential that you seek a small group or community of followers of Jesus to help you live with your commitment. Continuing in this series with other Jesus-followers will be very important as we all grow in intimacy with Him.

welcome to the family of God!

When we begin our relationship with Jesus, we become members of God's family. He makes extraordinary changes in our lives and in the lives of people around us as we grow in Him and learn to live like Him!

Through following Christ, we become His disciples. Being a disciple is similar to being a student. We don't know everything about our heavenly Father, but we're on our way to learning and experiencing this Christlike life. This will be an exciting time of growth for us all. From here let's commit to growing together in our relationship with God our Father, Jesus His Son, and the Holy Spirit.

how to use this book

This book can be used with a group, or by a person wanting to move through this process alone. If you are doing this alone, simply read through each section, pausing to reflect on each question or comment you see in italics. Write your thoughts here in this book, as you'll likely want to read them again at a later date to see how you've made progress as you learn to share your faith. You'll need only this book, a pen or pencil, and a Bible.

If you're doing this book with a group, you'll read through the sections aloud, and then pause to discuss the questions that are in italics. Again, group members will want to write their thoughts and reflections to read again as they are growing in their abilities to share their faith. Each person will need a copy of this book, a pen or pencil, and a Bible.

If you're the one leading a small group through this book, you'll find additional helps later in the book. We've provided an optional discussion-starter or activity that will engage your group as you begin each session. Use these if you'd like. You'll also find additional helps on how to lead a group. See the table of contents to find these additional sections in the book.

Entering a Relationship with God

>> Look! I stand at the door and knock. If you hear my voice and open the door, I will come in, and will share a meal together as friends. (Revelation 3:20)

following Jesus

Being a Christ-follower is unique. It's a relationship rather than a religion, an experience of family rather than a set of rituals. All around the world there are lonely people desperate to find relationships with others and a god figure who will meet their needs. Often they'll do anything to get friends to like them and their gods to accept them.

God already loves us and wants to have a deep and caring relationship with us. But there is nothing we can do to *earn* that loving relationship. The never-ending close relationship with God is the privilege of followers of Jesus. It is a *free gift* that comes through our faith and love in Christ Jesus. This is our story joined with God's story, and it's different from any religion. God's gift of eternal life is not something we can earn by being rich or by doing good works. It does seem impossible to think that we could come to know God personally without having to earn this friendship. But Jesus said, "Humanly speaking, it is impossible. But not with God. Everything is possible with God" (Mark 10:27).

Faith Journey

a starting point

Then he brought them out and asked, "Sirs, what must I do to be saved?"
They replied, "Believe in the Lord Jesus and you will be saved, along with everyone in your household."
(Acts 16:30-31)

At the beginning of this relationship, here's what's needed on your part:

- A desire to know and please God.
- Humbly admitting your selfish life outside of God's desire for you.
- Believing in all that Jesus said and did.
- Accepting and trusting Jesus to be your Savior and Lord.

continuing the relationship

Every relationship requires attention to keep it in good shape. None of us stays friends with anyone very long if we ignore the friend. It's the same with God. We can maintain our relationship with God by doing these things:

- Living with others in humility and service, demonstrating our love for them and Jesus.
- Spending time with Jesus in prayer and reading the Bible.
- Sharing God's story through our faith, our lifestyle, and our example.

understanding more about this relationship

Let's read some sections of the Bible to find out more about our relationship with Jesus. Read the verses and answer the questions below each one. If you're working in a group, discuss the questions together.

Read Ephesians 2:1-10.
What does this passage tell us about the gift of grace?

What does it tell us about salvation?

If our salvation is a gift, then why should we make the effort to grow or learn more?

Is there any reason for living a good life and doing good deeds? Explain your answer.

Read Luke 2:52.
What example did Jesus set for us with His own life?

What are the four areas in which He grew, and how would you put these into your own words?

How are you growing in each of these areas?

Read Romans 12:1-2.
How would you put these verses into your own words?

What is one thing you could do to apply this passage to your own life?

Read 2 Corinthians 5:20.
How can we encourage others to come to Jesus?

What do you think it means to be an ambassador of Jesus?

Read Ephesians 4 and 5.
What are a few of the key ideas from these chapters?

What do you learn from these chapters about living as a follower of Jesus?

DO THIS AT HOME THIS WEEK

Now it's time to reflect on your own relationship with Christ. Reflect on these questions and write down your thoughts. Later, share your answers with others in your group.

What changes have taken place in my life since I accepted Jesus as my Savior?

In what ways can others see changes in me?

What can others see in my life that might make them want to have a relationship with God?

What am I doing to maintain and strengthen my relationship with God?

Read "Becoming a Loving Parent" beginning on page 101 of this book.

Faith Journey

PRAYER TIME

- Pray that the Lord will help you seek to grow in your relationship with Jesus.
- Pray that the Lord will lead you in sharing your story and God's story about Jesus with others.
- Pray that your life will reflect Jesus to others.

MEMORY VERSE

Look! I stand at the door and knock. If you hear my voice and open the door, I will come in, and will share a meal together as friends. (Revelation 3:20)

Who Is God?

>> We know how much God loves us, and we have put our
trust in his love. God is love, and all who live in love
live in God, and God lives in them. (1 John 4:16)

knowing God

If we want to grow in our relationship with God and learn to live more like Jesus, we must first know who God is. As we learn who He is, we'll grow in our faith. So by putting Him first and learning about His character, we'll eventually develop a character shaped by His.

If we only try to have good character but don't have a close relationship with Jesus, we may learn how to be good (moral) people but not have the life of Jesus within us. Goodness and godliness are not the same thing. The first priority is to become a godly man or woman (a person with an intimate relationship with Jesus), not just a "good" man or woman (a person with good morals). Good deeds and right behavior will come as a result of our relationship with God and walking in obedience to His Word. *Knowing Him* is the beginning of this relationship. Let's take time during this session to look at a few important lessons about God.

the trinity

The first lesson about God is: God is one, yet He has three distinct persons. Followers of Jesus use the word *Trinity* to describe God.

God is one; He is one (singular) in His being and His purpose. He is unified in all of His characteristics, yet He has three distinct persons: Father, Son, and Holy Spirit, which become apparent in the roles He performs.

Now, if that sounds a bit confusing, don't be discouraged. This can be a very difficult concept to grasp! Below is an illustration that will help us understand the Trinity just a little bit.

Think about the sun. The sun is just one object in the sky, yet it has three very important functions. It gives light. It also gives heat. Finally, the same sun gives energy, which is used in place of electricity. This same sun has three functions or roles.

This simple illustration can help us understand the Trinity just a little more — one God who is described as three persons with three distinct roles. He is a Father, a Son, and the Holy Spirit.

Theologians (people who study God and the Bible) have been trying to understand this since Jesus came to us, and while they have very good ideas and descriptions, this remains one of the marvelous mysteries of God.

Here are some important points to remember:

1. All three persons are God (not people). Look up the following verses and write down what each tells us about God.

God the Father: 2 Corinthians 1:3

God the Son: John 1:1 and 14 (In these verses "Word" refers to Jesus.)

God the Holy Spirit: John 15:26

2. There are not three Gods, but one God.

3. The three persons are all in agreement and work in harmony together. There is no fighting or division among them.

God's character

In order to understand God and how He works in our lives, we must grow in our understanding of His character. We must understand that God is the same yesterday, today, and forever. He has never and will never go against His nature. His personality, character, and attributes do not change.

As humans with limited capacity to understand, it can be difficult to grasp the whole character and nature of God. Thankfully, our God wants us to know Him—so He has opened the way, through Jesus, for us to get to know Him. God is perfect, lacking nothing, all-knowing, all-present, all-powerful, eternal, and unchanging.

Here are more verses you can look up about the Trinity. After you look these up, write out any questions you have and ask your leader about them.

- John 1:1-4
- John 10:30
- John 14:11-13,16-18
- John 16:13-15
- John 17:5,11
- 1 Timothy 3:16

From what you already know of God, what do you know of His character?

One way we can learn more about God's character is by studying the names of God in the Bible. There can be a lot of meaning in a name. Parents often think deeply over what names to give their children when they're born. They want the name to be special—a name with meaning and honor. In the same way, the names the Lord has given to Himself help us understand more about His character.

Read the following passages and identify some of the names God has given to Himself.

Isaiah 43:3

1 John 1:5

1 John 4:16

Faith Journey

Revelation 1:17

Matthew 1:23

Psalm 95

Jesus Christ is the same yesterday, today, and forever. (Hebrews 13:8)

What do these names mean for you as a friend of God?

What's your favorite name for God? Why?

truths about God

Sometimes people have a wrong understanding of God, which can mislead and hinder them as they seek to grow in their journeys with Jesus. For example, if we don't believe that God is forgiving, we may allow guilt to continue to weigh us down. So it's important that we know what is true about God.

Like all relationships, the best way to get to know someone is to spend time with them. It's important to spend time getting to know God through prayer and time studying the Bible. Time spent with God will help us grow in our understanding of who He really is. It will help us to know and understand His unchanging, consistent, loving character.

Read the following passages and write the truths that you learn about God from each one:

Isaiah 40:28

Psalm 59:17

Romans 5:5-11

Psalm 90:2

Jeremiah 23:24

Jeremiah 32:17

James 1:17

1 John 3:20

Which of these means the most to you? Why?

God is love

We were created in love, to be in a love relationship with God. Unfortunately, God's perfect love is often misunderstood because our culture has changed what love really means. God's love is perfect and is not conditional on our good behavior—we don't need to do anything to make Him love us. He loves us because He is Love, love is His whole being, and He created us out of His love.

Read 1 Corinthians 13.
How is love defined? Is love in this passage an emotion or feeling, or is it an action? Explain.

What do you learn about God from this chapter?

What do you learn for your own life that you can apply?

God's example for us to follow

Genesis 1:26 says, "Then God said, 'Let us make human beings in our image, to be like us.'"

God wants us to be like Him and reflect Him to others. Read the following verses and note what you learn about God. Then write what should be seen in your life, as you are created in God's image, to be like Him.

Deuteronomy 7:9

Psalm 119:137

Psalm 130:3-4

1 Peter 1:15-16

1 John 1:5

1 John 4:16

In our growth as followers of Jesus, we'll learn more and more about God's nature and His attributes. However, it's important that we learn what is truth and not error. God is everywhere and does not hide Himself from His children. He has provided a way for us to know Him more deeply through the Bible, as well as through the example of Jesus' life and teachings. The Bible says that even all of creation testifies to the nature and glory of God.

DO THIS AT HOME THIS WEEK

Read 1 Chronicles 29:10-13.
David's prayer highlights many things about God. Following David's example, write a prayer to God, praising Him for who He is and what He is like.

Faith Journey

What part of knowing God seems most confusing to you right now? Write that here, and then make time to talk to a Christian leader about it this week.

What's one exciting thing you've learned about God through this session? How does this new truth change your relationship with God?

What can you do this week to show others the image of God through your life?

PRAYER TIME

- Pray that the Lord will continue to show Himself to you, and that you'll grow closer each day.
- Pray that you'll continue to grow in being godly and reflecting God's image to others.

MEMORY VERSE

I, yes I, am the LORD, and there is no other Savior. (Isaiah 43:11)

God the Father

>> For ever since the world was created, people have seen
the earth and sky. Through everything God made, they
can clearly see his invisible qualities—his eternal
power and divine nature. So they have no excuse for not
knowing God. (Romans 1:20)

a story of a loving father

Lekita was a young Masai moran whose time for initiation into manhood had arrived. He was the oldest son in his family and would be the one to carry on his father's name. Lekita and his father were very close, and there was no doubt that they loved each other.

According to the Masai culture, a boy would become a man after his father took him at sunset to a lonely, lion-inhabited forest far away from home. The young boy was then abandoned in the forest for the night until the next morning. If he survived the night, he would be brought home for a victorious initiation ceremony. Sadly, lions sometimes attacked and killed the boys.

Since Lekita's father loved him so much, he feared for his son's life, yet he had no choice but to let his son graduate to manhood. The pain of abandoning his son in the lion-infested forest was haunting, so Lekita's father decided to climb a tree a short distance away where he could watch over his son throughout the night.

Lekita was incredibly terrified and felt abandoned, especially by his father.

How could a truly loving father throw him mercilessly to hungry lions? But as far as Lekita could understand, that's exactly what his father had done. Lekita did not know that his father was right there with him in the cold, lonely forest—so far yet so near!

Have you ever felt that God was far away in the unknown, beyond your reach? Like Lekita's father, God is keenly watching over us to ensure that we'll be safe in Him. He is a loving Father who wants the best for us.

God is our father

What comes to mind when you hear the word *father*? Write your thoughts here, or if you're working in a group, discuss your thoughts together.

For some people, *father* brings to mind a loving, caring parent or relative who played an important role in their development and lives. For others, *father* brings to mind bad memories of a parent or relative who was cruel and abusive.

Then there are those who don't know how to describe *father* because they never had a father or father figure in their lives.

What characteristics do most children want their parents to display the most?

What characteristics do *you* want your parents to display the most?

God, our heavenly Father, is perfect in all His ways. He will far exceed any expectations we have of our earthly parents.

What does this mean to you?

God, the perfect father

We know what our ideal parent would be like. Let's look at some aspects of God our heavenly Father's character and consider what it means to have God as our Father.

God Is Present with Us in Every Circumstance

Read these verses below and write what they say about our heavenly Father.
Deuteronomy 31:6-8

Psalm 121:8

Psalm 139:7-11

Psalm 125:2

How is God present in your life? Give specific examples.

How do you feel about a Father who is with you every moment? Explain your thoughts.

If God the Father is present in every circumstance, then we can trust that we're never alone. He will not abandon us nor neglect us. If we don't feel like He's near, we need to remember God's promise from Deuteronomy 31:6: "So be strong and courageous! Do not be afraid and do not panic before them. For the LORD your God will personally go ahead of you. He will neither fail you nor abandon you."

God Provides for Our Needs

Read the following verses and note what is said about our Father's loving provision for us.
Matthew 7:7-11

Luke 12:22-32

How have you seen God provide for you in your own life?

How have you seen God meet the needs of others you know?

What are some specific needs that you want God to provide?

God Performs Great Wonders

The Bible is full of miracles and wonders that God has performed throughout time. God continues to do great things for all of us, His children, even today.

Read the following verses and note what God did.

Genesis 1:1

Psalm 77:11-14

Psalm 65:5-8

Romans 1:20

What miracles or wonders have you seen God perform in your life?

What miracles have you seen God do in the lives of others you know? In your community? In your nation?

Our Father does wonderful miracles—large and small. Creation and everything around us testifies to the wonders of God. As we observe His wonders, we'll begin to see and appreciate more and more of His character. The next time you see a glorious sunset or hear a bird sing or notice a flower growing in a dry place, you can stop and thank God for those precious performances of His creativity and love.

God Pursues Us with Great Energy

Read the following passages and note how God pursues us, wanting us to be His.
Matthew 18:12-14

Luke 15:8-10

Luke 19:10

What do these words mean to you? How do you feel knowing you are this important to your Father?

God our Father desires to be a part of our lives. He does not remain aloof and distant, but instead *pursues* us. He cares about our lives and wants a relationship with us. He will not push Himself on us, but is always seeking after us.

How do we see God still seeking after us?

DO THIS AT HOME THIS WEEK

Take some time to reflect on the four statements below. Write below each one what this means to you to have a Father like this.

God is present with us in every circumstance.

God provides our needs.

God performs great wonders for us.

God pursues us with great energy.

Read "God the Father—A True Story" beginning on page 103 of this book. Consider what it means to you to have God as your Father. Write your own true story.

PRAYER TIME

This week, write your prayer using this prayer below as a guide:

Dear God,

Thank you for being my Father. I especially thank you for being present in these situations of my life . . .

I also thank you for providing these needs . . .

I thank you for performing great things for me (write some specific things here).

Thank you for persisting with me and bringing me to salvation and now teaching me more about yourself. I commit myself to looking and listening to you and obeying your plan for my life.

Your child,

MEMORY VERSE

The Lord keeps you from all harm and watches over your life. The Lord keeps watch over you as you come and go, both now and forever. (Psalm 121:7-8)

The Father and You

>> Look at the birds. They don't plant or harvest or store food in barns, for your heavenly Father feeds them. And aren't you far more valuable to him than they are? (Matthew 6:26)

God created us

Our heavenly Father created us to be unique. He loves us so much that He made us all individuals with our own feelings, personalities, character, looks, and abilities. He loves all of us as He created us to be. We're all very special!

This session will help us understand more about our relationship with God as our Father and let us know more about who we are to God.
Read Psalm 139 and then reflect on these questions. If you're in a group, discuss them together.

Do you think God took great care in creating you? Why or why not?

Has this psalm changed your feelings about any part of your body, your abilities, or anything else about you? If so, what?

What does it mean to you that God created you Himself?

Other verses that remind us that God created us are Isaiah 43:1 and Genesis 1:26-27.

God knows us

According to Psalm 139:1-4, what does God know about our lives?

If God knows us so intimately, can we hide anything from Him? What does that mean to you?

Would you like Psalm 139:23-24 to be a prayer for your own life? Why or why not?

What does it mean to you that God truly knows you inside and out?

God loves us

What's the greatest way God has shown His love to you?

Read John 3:16. What did God do out of His love for the whole world? What is so significant about this to you? Can you imagine anyone else doing this for you?

A father looks after his children just as a shepherd watches over his sheep. God describes Himself as a Shepherd and us as His sheep. Read Ezekiel 34:11-16 and Psalm 23.

In what ways do these verses show us how God cares?

How do you feel knowing the God of all the universe loves you?

God made you a part of his family

According to John 1:12-14, how are you born into God's family?

Who does Romans 8:15 say God is? What does this verse say about us? (Did you know that *abba* means "daddy"?)

List some of the advantages of being a true child of God from Romans 8:15-17.

What does it mean to you to be a part of your own physical family?

What do you think the idea of family is like?

How is being a part of God's family significant?

It is important for us to *know* that God is our Father and that we have eternal life. We cannot depend on our *feelings* to know this; rather, this assurance must come from the Word of God. Spend time reading and learning the Word of God so that it will be fresh in your mind and will help you overcome any doubts you may have about being a child of God.

DO THIS AT HOME THIS WEEK

- Read these verses and put your own name into it. What does it mean to you when it's so personal?

Even before he made the world, God loved [your name] and chose [your name] in Christ to be holy and without fault in his eyes. God decided in advance to adopt [your name] into his own family by bringing [your name] to himself through Jesus Christ. This is what he wanted to do, and it gave him great pleasure. (Ephesians 1:4-5)

- Read "I Am Your Father" beginning on page 105 of this book.
- Every day this week, tell two people that God loves them. At the end of each day, write down what happened when you did this.

PRAYER TIME

Lord, I praise you because you made me! Out of your love, you formed me and all my days have been prearranged by you. Father, help me to believe how wonderfully I've been made by you. Help me to love others and myself as you love me. Thank you, Father, for creating me to be your child. Amen.

MEMORY VERSE

Look at the birds. They don't plant or harvest or store food in barns, for your heavenly Father feeds them. And aren't you far more valuable to him than they are? (Matthew 6:26)

The Son of God

>> But the angel reassured them. "Don't be afraid!" he said. "I bring you good news that will bring great joy to all people. The Savior—yes, the Messiah, the Lord—has been born today in Bethlehem, the city of David!" (Luke 2:10-11)

who is Jesus?

The coming of the Son of God, our Savior, was foretold for hundreds of years. It was fulfilled with the birth of Jesus Christ the Lord.

Jesus is unique because He is completely God while also completely man. Being both divine and human, He is able to be the perfect sacrifice to take the punishment for our sin. As God He was perfect, and only a perfect sacrifice would be sufficient to pay for everyone's rebellion against God. As a human being He experienced terrible suffering, hanging nailed to the cross for all the people of the world, including us. Though He lived a normal human life, complete with temptations and many good and bad life experiences, He was able to overcome everything to show us how we can live in every situation.

Many of us have heard the Christmas story, but it's great to refresh ourselves on the facts, directly from the Bible. Read Luke 1:26-45; 2:1-20 to learn exactly what happened.

Jesus is God

Let's look directly to the Bible for evidence of who Jesus is.
Look up Philippians 2:6-11. List at least four things this verse says about Jesus Christ.

Read these verses and answer the questions below.

> For God made Christ, who never sinned, to be the offering for our sin, so that we could be made right with God through Christ. (2 Corinthians 5:21)

What would it take for a person to never sin? Do you think this is one way Jesus is proved to be God? Explain.

> Jesus Christ is the same yesterday, today, and forever. (Hebrews 13:8)

We know that God is unchanging. Does this statement about Jesus help to show you that He is God? Why or why not?

The Son of God

> God created everything through him, and nothing was created except through him. (John 1:3)

What does this mean?

How does it help show Jesus as God?

> He also says to the Son, "In the beginning, Lord, you laid the foundation of the earth and made the heavens with your hands. They will perish, but you remain forever. They will wear out like old clothing. You will fold them up like a cloak and discard them like old clothing. But you are always the same; you will live forever." (Hebrews 1:10-12)

How does the eternal nature of Jesus reflect who He is?

Read Galatians 4:4-7 and put it into your own words.

Why did God send His Son?

What are we called in this passage? What does that mean?

We also know that Jesus is God through His miracles. Read Mark 2:3-12 and Matthew 14:22-33. The miracles that Jesus performed defied the laws of nature. In the eyes of the people, He had done what was said to be impossible. For Christ, miracles were not difficult at all—they were totally within His power. As God, Jesus could do anything and everything—even defy the laws of nature. For example, walking on water was not impossible for Him.

the sacrifice Jesus made for us

We're all valuable to God. We're so valuable that He was willing to pay an enormous price for our salvation. He paid the price with His own life. We're all valuable to God and we can live with a sense of worth because of what Jesus has done for us all.

Read John 17, Jesus' prayer to the Father just before He was arrested and then crucified.

This prayer can be broken into three sections. In your own words, what did the Son of God ask the Father to do?

Verses 1-5

Verses 6-19

Verses 20-26

What does this prayer mean to you personally?

Read Hebrews 2:14-16. Spend some time answering the following questions:
What happened when Jesus became a man?

What do you understand as the Son of God's ultimate sacrifice for you?

How does this make you feel?

How do you want your life to reflect your relationship with Jesus?

DO THIS AT HOME THIS WEEK

- Read John 1:1-18 and note what you learn here about Jesus being God.
- Read "The Son" beginning on page 107 of this book.
- Read the poem, "The Son Light," on the following page. Write your own poem of praise to the Son of God for who He is.

The Son Light
The sun shines
The Son is the light
The sun is natural and mortal
The Son is eternal, the source of life
The sun is always there, trustworthy
The Son never leaves me, he lives within me
The sun is my natural light
The Son is my Saviour

The Son is my guide
He lives within
He loves me, cares for me
Died for me, prays for me

The Son became flesh
That I might be born anew in spirit
He became sin that I might be free
The Son is the Breath of Life

The Son is the Lord of Life
The Son is the Source of Life
The Son is Life
And gave himself for me

He is the Son
And loves me so much
He brought me to his Father
And I became a child of God

—Ayo Ipinmoye

PRAYER TIME

- Thank Jesus for interceding before God the Father on your behalf.
- Pray that the Lord will deepen your relationship with Jesus.
- Pray you'll grow in your knowledge and understanding of the Son of God.

MEMORY VERSE

Now I am departing from the world; they are staying in this world, but I am coming to you. Holy Father, you have given me your name; now protect them by the power of your name so that they will be united just as we are. (John 17:11)

Jesus as Man and Savior

>> For a child is born to us, a son is given to us.
The government will rest on his shoulders.
And he will be called: Wonderful Counselor,
Mighty God, Everlasting Father, Prince of Peace.
(Isaiah 9:6)

Jesus was a human man

God promised a Son who would be given to redeem the world. This promise was given during the time of the prophet Isaiah, generations before the actual birth of Jesus. There was eager expectation as the people awaited the birth of the anointed one — the Christ.

God's love can be seen in the fact that Jesus came to earth as an infant. This placed Him in a very vulnerable position. An infant is totally defenseless and cannot survive on its own. It must be taken care of and protected by its parents.

Jesus experienced life on earth — He learned to walk and talk. He experienced the heat of summer and the cold of winter. He felt pain, sadness, anger, happiness, joy, and suffering. In all ways physical, mental, and emotional He experienced life as a man, but He was also God.

Faith Journey

Jesus Had Earthly Parents and Was a Boy

Read Luke 2:46-51 and answer the following questions. If you're working in a group, discuss these together.

This is a situation many children have had—being separated from their parents and the parents being worried. What about Jesus' answer surprises you?

What do you think it might have been like for Jesus growing up as a boy?

According to Luke 2:52, in what areas of life did Jesus grow?

How are these similar to growth in your own life?

Jesus Had Human Needs and Feelings

How is Jesus' humanity revealed in the following passages?
Mark 4:38

Luke 22:43-44

John 4:7

John 11:35

Jesus Was Tempted

Like all humans, Jesus was tempted. Read Matthew 4:1-11. Jesus had an answer to each temptation Satan presented.

Temptation 1: What was Jesus' answer? What does this mean?

Temptation 2: What was Jesus' answer? What does this mean?

Temptation 3: What was Jesus' answer? What does this mean?

What does it mean to be tempted? Share one temptation you often face.

Jesus resisted temptation. What can we learn from His example?

Based on Jesus' example, what can we do to fight against temptation?

Temptation in and of itself is not wrong. If we give in to temptation, then we fail. Temptation entices us to leave God's protection and live outside His will for us. This can be very serious. If we give in to some temptations, we could suffer broken relationships and injury, maybe even death.

Jesus is our savior

Even though Jesus was God's Son, he learned obedience from the things he suffered. In this way, God qualified him as a perfect High Priest, and he became the source of eternal salvation for all those who obey him. (Hebrews 5:8-9)

The reality is we all have fallen short of the standards God has set for us. Our rebellion, or sin, comes in many different ways: through doing things we're told not to do, through damaging what is good (like the environment or relationships), through not doing what we know we should do, and through pretending or trying to be something we're not.

Sin is sin. There is no one who has ever lived who has not offended God in one way or another. Because of our rebellion, no one could have access to God. We are all cut off and doomed to eternal separation from God, but Jesus came and died on our behalf so that we might be acceptable to our heavenly Father. Jesus is our Savior.

Read the following verses and name what we are saved from through Jesus:

Romans 6:23

Romans 6:14

Revelation 21:1-5

Acts 4:12 says, "There is salvation in no one else! God has given no other name under heaven by which we must be saved."
How does this verse help you answer those who say there are many ways to be saved or many ways to heaven?

God the son forgives us through his death

Look up the following verses and answer the questions that follow.

- 1 Peter 3:18
- Romans 5:6-7
- Colossians 2:13-14

What did Jesus do for us? Do you think it was easy for Him? Why or why not?

What did His death accomplish for us?

Would you expect someone who had never done anything wrong to give up His life for you? Why or why not?

God the son frees us through his resurrection

Look up the following verses and answer the questions that follow.

- 2 Corinthians 5:18-21
- John 8:34-36
- Romans 8:1-2

What is the result of Jesus being raised from the dead?

What are the implications for your life?

What does being "free" mean to you personally?

> Christ suffered for [your name]'s sins once for all time. He never sinned, but he died for sinners to bring [your name] safely home to God. He suffered physical death, but he was raised to life in the Spirit. (1 Peter 3:18)

DO THIS AT HOME THIS WEEK

As a Christian, there are a number of words that you'll hear people use to describe Jesus and what He's done for you. Look up these words and write a simple definition that you can easily understand for each one.

Salvation

Savior

Atone

Redeemer

Resurrection

Cross

Guilt

Assurance

PRAYER TIME

Lord Jesus, thank you for the sacrifice you made so that I might have eternal life. Thank you for the gifts of forgiveness, freedom from death, and the Bible. Help me live every day in a manner that is pleasing to you. Help me never to forget all that you have done for me. I love you, Lord Jesus. Amen.

MEMORY VERSE

God showed how much he loved us by sending his one and only Son into the world so that we might have eternal life through him. This is real love — not that we loved God, but that he loved us and sent his Son as a sacrifice to take away our sins. (1 John 4:9-10)

God the Holy Spirit

>> But when the Father sends the Advocate as my representative—that is, the Holy Spirit—he will teach you everything and will remind you of everything I have told you. (John 14:26)

For God has not given us a spirit of fear and timidity, but of power, love, and self-discipline. (2 Timothy 1:7)

the promise of the Holy Spirit

Jesus did not want to leave His disciples without help. He said that the Father would send a helper to teach, guide, and direct them while He returned to the Father. That helper is the Holy Spirit. The Spirit is one with the Father and the Son, and is the third person of the Trinity.
Read the following passages and answer the questions that follow.

- John 14:16-17,26
- John 15:26-27
- John 16:7-15

What did Jesus promise in these passages?

What is an "advocate"?

Explain in your own words what Jesus says about the Holy Spirit.

the work of the Holy Spirit

The Holy Spirit works in and through the lives of believers in many ways. We may not know when or how the Spirit will work through and in us, but if we're available we can be assured that the Spirit of God will use us to reach out to others for Christ.

Read the following verses and answer the questions below.

- Romans 8:9
- 1 Corinthians 2:12
- 1 Corinthians 3:16
- Titus 3:5-6
- Galatians 4:6

How does the Holy Spirit help those who are followers of Jesus?

How do you see the Holy Spirit doing these things in your own life now?

How would you like to see the Holy Spirit become more active in your life?

the coming of the Holy Spirit

Jesus had promised that the Holy Spirit would come after He returned to heaven. Acts 1:8 says, "But you will receive power when the Holy Spirit comes upon you. And you will be my witnesses, telling people about me everywhere — in Jerusalem, throughout Judea, in Samaria, and to the ends of the earth."

After Jesus ascended into heaven, the disciples gathered in Jerusalem to await the promised arrival of the Holy Spirit. They did not know when or how the Spirit would come, but they trusted the promise Jesus made that the Father would send a helper. The Holy Spirit came as promised, and the Spirit's presence transformed the lives of those gathered in the Upper Room. For example, Peter — the apostle who denied Jesus three times and then fled — spoke boldly to the people. He strongly proclaimed Christ. The one who denied became the one who proclaimed by the power of the Holy Spirit.

Read Acts 2 for the account of what happened when this promise was fulfilled.

living under the Holy Spirit's control

In Acts 1:8, Jesus used the expression "you will" twice. He made both of these statements in reference to the coming of the Holy Spirit.

What two statements did He make?

How does the Holy Spirit help us in telling others about Jesus?

What were some of the disciples' activities after being filled with the Holy Spirit (Acts 2:42)?

Whom does the Holy Spirit glorify (John 16:13-14)?

What is one activity in which the Holy Spirit helps us, according to Romans 8:26?

What are the two conflicting natures in our lives (Galatians 5:16-17)?

What is the "sword" of the Spirit (Ephesians 6:17)?

What effect does the Word of God have on the follower of Jesus (Hebrews 4:12; Romans 12:1)?

being Spirit-filled

Sometimes people will say that Christians need to live a "Spirit-filled" life. Simply put, this means:

- A life of obedience to the Holy Spirit.
- A life centered on a relationship with Jesus Christ.
- A life founded on God's Word, the Bible.
- A life of prayer.
- A life of relationships with other Christians.
- A life of witness, sharing the love of Jesus with others who don't yet know Him.

DO THIS AT HOME THIS WEEK

Study the following Scripture passages that highlight the attributes of God's Holy Spirit. Beside each passage, write what you learn about the Holy Spirit.

- Hebrews 9:14
- Psalm 139:7-13
- 1 Corinthians 2:10
- Luke 1:35; Romans 15:19
- 1 Peter 4:14
- Genesis 1:26-27; Job 33:4
- Matthew 28:19; 2 Corinthians 13:14
- John 3:5,6; 1 John 5:4
- Acts 2:24; 1 Peter 3:18; Hebrews 13:20; Romans 1:4
- 2 Timothy 3:16; 2 Peter 1:21
- 1 Corinthians 12:8; Isaiah 11:2; John 16:13; John 14:26
- John 14:47; 1 Corinthians 14:25; 1 Corinthians 3:16; 1 Corinthians 6:19

PRAYER TIME

- Pray that you might grow to understand who the Spirit is and the role the Holy Spirit plays in your life.
- Pray that you'll hear the Holy Spirit guiding you in your walk with Jesus.

MEMORY VERSE

And I will ask the Father, and he will give you another Advocate, who will never leave you. He is the Holy Spirit, who leads into all truth. (John 14:16-17)

The Holy Spirit and Us

>> And I will give them singleness of heart and put a
new spirit within them. I will take away their stony,
stubborn heart and give them a tender, responsive heart,
so they will obey my decrees and regulations. Then they
will truly be my people, and I will be their God. (Ezekiel
11:19-20)

the Spirit convinces us of the truth

God is the Life-Giving Spirit, continually at work in our lives. The Spirit does this primarily by changing our hearts. Let's explore what this means.
In John 16:12-13 Jesus says, "There is so much more I want to tell you, but you can't bear it now. When the Spirit of truth comes, he will guide you into all truth. He will not speak on his own but will tell you what he has heard. He will tell you about the future."

What do you think it means to be guided into all truth?

What else does Jesus say the Spirit will do?

The primary way in which the Holy Spirit speaks to followers of Jesus is through Scripture. The Bible is God's Word and is complete. In this manner, the Holy Spirit will confirm the truth to us. Sometimes the Spirit will open our eyes in a new way and reveal Bible passages to us, giving us understanding and insight into God's Word.

the Spirit corrects us and renews us when we go wrong

Read John 16:5-15.

The Lord created people with a free will to make their own choices. He also created each person with a conscience. Do you hear a "voice" when you're about to do something that you know is wrong? That's the voice of the Holy Spirit prompting your conscience.

Do you feel uneasy when your friends try to convince you to go along with them when you know they're going to be unkind or do something that would displease God? The "bad feeling" that you have comes from the Spirit and is warning you that you should listen.

The Holy Spirit is continually communicating with us and correcting us.

In what ways do you "hear" or "sense" the Holy Spirit correcting you and helping you mend your ways?

Are there times when you don't listen? Discuss this and share about what gets in the way of listening.

Be sure to ask the Holy Spirit to forgive you, and commit yourself to listening more intently to His guiding.

the Spirit comforts us in our daily living

In John 14:16 Jesus says, "And I will ask the Father, and he will give you another Advocate, who will never leave you."

The word *advocate* also means "comforter," "counselor," or "encourager."

How could you use the comfort of the Holy Spirit? The counsel? The encouragement?

the Spirit counsels us

We already know from John 14:26 that the Spirit is a counselor. John 15:26 is another place that the word Advocate, or Counselor, is used. In this verse Jesus says, "But I will send you the Advocate — the Spirit of truth. He will come to you from the Father and will testify all about me."

The counsel of the Holy Spirit will guide us in all that we need to know. Specifically, we can rely on the Holy Spirit to counsel us toward a:

- Deeper knowledge of God.
- Deeper relationship with Jesus.
- Deeper commitment to tell others the gospel of Jesus Christ.

the fruit of the Spirit

When we accept Jesus as Lord, the Father sends the Holy Spirit to help us in our walk with Jesus. As the Spirit comes into our lives, we begin to be transformed in our character. Among other things, the Holy Spirit helps produce fruit in our lives.

In John 15:5 Jesus says, "Yes, I am the vine; you are the branches. Those who remain in me, and I in them, will produce much fruit. For apart from me you can do nothing."

Have you ever met someone and known from the moment you were introduced that something was different about that person, only later to find out that the person is a Jesus-follower? The Holy Spirit's transforming presence is what you sensed. The Spirit produces fruit in the lives of all who follow Jesus. The fruit of the Spirit is the nature and behavior that the Holy Spirit produces in all those people in whom the Spirit dwells and works.

Read Galatians 5:16-25.

Which of the "desires of your sinful nature" do you most struggle with? You don't have to share these aloud if you're not comfortable, but do privately identify them.

Take some time and examine who you were before becoming a follower of Jesus and who you've become since accepting Jesus and living by the Spirit. Second Corinthians 5:17 says, "This means that anyone who belongs to Christ has become a new person. The old life is gone; a new life has begun!"

How exciting to know that God's Spirit can give us the strength to turn from these old ways and give us a new life as a new person!

As you look at Galatians 5:22-23 you'll see the fruit of the Spirit listed. Explain how this fruit might be demonstrated in someone's life.

What part do we play in allowing the Holy Spirit to produce fruit in our lives?

What fruit has the Holy Spirit produced in your life since you became a follower of Jesus?

the gifts of the Spirit

Read 1 Corinthians 12:1-12; Romans 12:4-13; and Ephesians 4:11-12.

The gifts of the Spirit are supernatural gifts and callings given to Jesus-followers by the Holy Spirit. There are many gifts. Some are for service and ministry, and others are spiritual gifts intended to enrich, encourage, and comfort the body of Christ. As it says in 1 Corinthians 12:7, "A spiritual gift is given to each of us so we can help each other."

What are a few of the gifts you see in the passages listed above?

Why are these gifts important?

What gifts do you think the Holy Spirit has given you? Explain.

DO THIS AT HOME THIS WEEK

- Think about the following statement and write your answer:

Right now, I need God's Spirit to counsel me, because . . .

- In working to be a responsible young follower of Jesus, personally identify the aspects of the fruit of the Spirit that are lacking in your life. Write these down and place them in a visible place to remind you to pray to the Lord to work in these areas of your life. Be sure to come back to these after a few weeks and evaluate how God is working in your life to change you.

PRAYER TIME

- Praise the Lord for the counsel and comfort of the Holy Spirit.
- Pray that God will guide you to use the gifts you've been given to help others.

MEMORY VERSE

But when the Father sends the Advocate as my representative — that is, the Holy Spirit — he will teach you everything and will remind you of everything I have told you. (John 14:26)

The Father, Son, and Holy Spirit

>> May the grace of the Lord Jesus Christ, the love of God, and the fellowship of the Holy Spirit be with you all. (2 Corinthians 13:14)

the trinity at work in our lives

We've spent many of the last sessions looking closer at each person of the Trinity. Let's take this session to go deeper into how the three are one, and how they work together.

- God the Father gives us a sense of significance because He has chosen to love us.
- God the Son gives us a sense of worth because He paid the enormous price to save us from the penalty of sin.
- God the Holy Spirit gives us a sense of strength because we're empowered to live a godly life on a daily basis in relationship with others.

Thus, we can see the three persons of the Trinity at work in us, giving us wholeness and completeness.

truth about the trinity

The word *Trinity* is not found in the Bible but is used to express the teaching of God in three persons—Father, Son (Jesus Christ), and Holy Spirit.

The truths taught about the Trinity are:

- That God is one and that there is one God (Deuteronomy 6:4; 1 Kings 8:60; Isaiah 44:6; Mark 12:29,32; John 10:30)
- That the Father is a distinct person, distinct from the Son and the Holy Spirit.
- That Jesus was and is truly God and yet was a person distinct from the Father and Holy Spirit.
- That the Holy Spirit is also a distinct, divine person and part of the Godhead.

three are one

Several places in the Bible refer to all three people of the Trinity. Read these verses and note which people of the Trinity are mentioned and in what context. If you're in a group, discuss these together.

Matthew 3:16-17

Matthew 28:19

Romans 8:9

1 Peter 1:2

the attributes of the trinity

We'll understand the Father, Son, and Holy Spirit and their work as one better if we learn more about their attributes or qualities. Read the verses that accompany each attribute, and notice specific examples of how that attribute is demonstrated and which person of the Trinity is being mentioned.

They're Eternal

This means they are everlasting, undying, unending, and timeless.
Romans 16:26

Revelation 22:13

Hebrews 9:14

They're Holy

Holy means to be righteous, sacred, or set apart.
Revelation 15:4

Acts 3:14

1 John 2:20

They're Omnipresent

To be omnipresent is to always be everywhere at the same time.
Jeremiah 23:24

Ephesians 1:23

Psalm 139:7

They're Omnipotent

This means they are all-powerful, having unlimited power.
Revelation 1:8

Romans 15:19

Jeremiah 32:17

Faith Journey

Hebrews 1:3

Luke 1:35

They're Omniscient

Someone who is omniscient is all-knowing.
Acts 15:18

John 21:17

1 Corinthians 2:10-11

They're Creator

Genesis 1:1

Colossians 1:16

Job 33:4

Psalm 148:5

John 1:3

Job 26:13

They're Teacher

Isaiah 54:13

Luke 21:15

John 14:26

Isaiah 48:17

Galatians 1:12

1 John 2:20

They're the Source of Eternal Life

It is only through God that we can experience eternal life in heaven. It is only through God that we can be saved.
Romans 6:23

John 10:28

Galatians 6:8

DO THIS AT HOME THIS WEEK

Consider all you've learned about the Trinity. What questions do you still have? Review the Bible passages we used this week to see if you can find your answers in the Bible. If you still have questions, make a time to talk to someone in leadership at your church to help you understand more clearly.

PRAYER TIME

- Thank the Father because you're significant and have a place in His kingdom.
- Thank the Son because you have worth.
- Thank the Spirit for the strength you've been given.

Faith Journey

MEMORY VERSE

God the Father knew you and chose you long ago, and his Spirit has made you holy. As a result, you have obeyed him and have been cleansed by the blood of Jesus Christ. (1 Peter 1:2)

Jesus as Lord

>> Therefore, God elevated him to the place of highest honor and gave him the name above all other names, that at the name of Jesus every knee should bow, in heaven and on earth and under the earth, and every tongue confess that Jesus Christ is Lord, to the glory of God the Father. (Philippians 2:9-11)

lord of our lives

In our culture today we don't use the term "lord" very often. It reminds us of past times when royalty was more common. Today we're more likely to think of supervisors, teachers, or others in positions of authority. But none of these positions commands the respect that the position of lord does. A lord truly is a ruler, and when we accept Jesus as the Lord of our life, we give Him all authority over us and willingly place Him in a position above us. We ask Him to rule our lives.

To grow as Christians, we must allow Jesus to be the Lord over all the areas of our lives. This means we do our best to put aside our desires and will, and instead follow the Lord's will. When we ask Jesus to be Lord of all the areas of our lives, we're asking Him to take control of our lives and lead us in the direction He wants for us.

This can be a very difficult component of any follower's life because even followers of Jesus can lack the faith to live as God would want them to. We need to continually be asking God to forgive us for trying to run our own lives and to daily give our lives to Him. The good thing is that Jesus promised in Matthew 11:28-30 to give us rest and make our burdens light. He also promised that when we're weak He is strong, and His strength is made perfect in our weakness (2 Corinthians 12:9-10). We just need the faith to believe this and to keep moving forward.

Jesus as lord

The Bible says Jesus Christ is Lord of all creation, both the living and the dead, and all His people (the church). (See Colossians 1:16-18 and Romans 14:9.)

Write your own definition of the word Lord as you think it applies to Jesus Christ.

Read these verses and answer the questions that follow.

- Philippians 2:9-11
- Hebrews 1:1-4

How do these verses describe Jesus?

What do these verses say happens in the presence of Jesus? How would this demonstrate that Jesus is Lord?

According to Colossians 1:18, what place should Jesus hold in the life of a believer?

What does this mean for your own life?

Read Romans 12:1.
What do you think this verse means?

How would putting this verse into action demonstrate to Jesus that you accept Him as Lord?

allow Jesus to be the lord of our lives

Every follower of Jesus has fears when it comes to surrendering his or her life to Jesus. What do you fear in giving your life over to Jesus? Complete this sentence: *I fear that . . .*

If you are in a group, share your fears together and encourage each other.

Another reason people may hold back from allowing Jesus to be the Lord of their lives is the thinking that Jesus doesn't really understand their problems. After all, He lived as a man a long time ago, and we may think He wouldn't understand life today. Put a mark beside each of the items below that you think may happen if you let Jesus be the Lord of your life:

- He may want me to do something I don't want to do.
- He may want me to enter a career I wouldn't enjoy.
- He might prevent me from getting married.
- He will take away my enjoyment of things I have, hobbies, or friends.
- He can help me in the "big" things, but He doesn't care about the little things.

What makes you think these things are true?

Now, what if He does do these things? Knowing that Jesus has all wisdom and knowledge, would you be willing to accept whatever He planned for your life, even if it meant that one of the things you marked did happen as a result of following Jesus?

Read Jeremiah 29:11.

How does this verse make you feel about your fears?

priorities in my life

Rank the following in order of the priority you give them in your life:

Family
Sleep
Friends
Jesus
Money
School
Hobbies
Belongings

Think about the way we set our priorities.
Does the amount of time you spend on each item justify the priority you give it?

Are there such things as godly priorities? If so, what might they be?

In Luke 6:46 Jesus said, "So why do you keep calling me 'Lord, Lord!' when you don't do what I say?"
Do you think Jesus might say this to you? Why or why not?

How do we know if Jesus Christ is truly the Lord of our lives?

DO THIS AT HOME THIS WEEK

- One day this week, keep a record of everything you do and the amount of time you spend on each activity. At the end of the day, look back at your list and see what priorities you gave to each thing based on how much time you spent on it. Were your priorities helpful in getting closer to Jesus? What could you have done differently?
- Read "Understanding Salvation" beginning on page 109 of this book.

PRAYER TIME

Ask the Lord to make you aware of the areas that you have not yet submitted to His Lordship. Write these down and continue to pray that God will help you give these areas over to Him.

MEMORY VERSE

Then he said to the crowd, "If any of you wants to be my follower, you must turn from your selfish ways, take up your cross daily, and follow me." (Luke 9:23)

Living Like Jesus

>> But you are not like that, for you are a chosen people. You are royal priests, a holy nation, God's very own possession. As a result, you can show others the goodness of God, for he called you out of the darkness into his wonderful light.

"Once you had no identity as a people; now you are God's people. Once you received no mercy; now you have received God's mercy."

Dear friends, I warn you as "temporary residents and foreigners" to keep away from worldly desires that wage war against your very souls. Be careful to live properly among your unbelieving neighbors. Then even if they accuse you of doing wrong, they will see your honorable behavior, and they will give honor to God when he judges the world. (1 Peter 2:9-12)

Have you ever wanted to be like someone else? Perhaps someone who was good at sports, or smart at school, or had a great sense of fashion? When you saw that person you'd think, *I wish I was more like him!* or *If only I had what she has!*

Through the previous sessions of this book we've focused a lot on knowing who God is. But how can we get to know Him more deeply? How can we say we have a personal relationship with Him?

Through the remainder of this book we'll learn how to study the Bible, how to pray and fast, and how to have quiet time with Jesus. These disciplines will help us to grow in our walk with Jesus.

Have you ever thought that maybe others want to be like *you*? That's one of the reasons why we want to live like Christ—so others will see what we've got in that relationship and want it too. God asks us to live a life like Jesus so that others too will want to know God and serve Him. By your example others can see Jesus.

In this session we're going to look closely at how to live like Jesus, and through that, honor God and draw others to Him.

love

One of the greatest ways to live like Jesus is to love others. In John 13:34 Jesus said, "So now I am giving you a new commandment: Love each other. Just as I have loved you, you should love each other." When Jesus spoke to His disciples about love, He wasn't teaching them about love as an *emotion*; He was speaking of love as an *action*.

Love should change the way we think and feel and *act* toward our parents, our teachers, our friends, our brothers and sisters, and even those who don't like us or those we'd consider our enemies. Love motivates us to seek the highest good for others. Love is the most powerful action that we can take. Remember it was the action of *love* that Jesus took when He allowed Himself to be nailed to the cross for us all.

To love as Jesus loves means putting others first, and this will show those around us that we really believe and live what we're saying. Jesus made it clear in John 13:35 that the way we treat each other will be the true test that we are His followers. That verse says, "Your love for one another will prove to the world that you are my disciples."

Read John 13:1-5 and 1 John 3:18, and then answer the following questions. If you're doing this in a group, discuss these together.

What do these verses teach us about love?

Think back on your actions in the past two hours. Would your actions show others that you love them? That you love Jesus? Why or why not?

a close relationship with God the father

Another way we can live like Jesus is to have a close relationship with God. Read John 14:7-15.

How do these verses show that Jesus had a close relationship with His Father?

obedience

Jesus always did the will of His Father, but it is also recorded that He was obedient to the wishes of His earthly parents.

Read Luke 2:46-51 and John 5:30.
What do these passages teach us about obedience to God?

To others in authority?

compassion

It's easy to ignore the multitude of needs we see around us, but as we learn from Christ's example, He did not turn away from the needs of others. He had consideration for them and was concerned about their every need. He showed compassion to others.

Read Matthew 9:35-38; Matthew 15:32-37; Mark 1:40-41; and Mark 5:32-34.

How did Jesus demonstrate compassion in each of these situations?

What did Jesus do that you *not* do?

What did Jesus do that you *could* do?

Think about the people close to you, such as family and friends. How can you show them compassion?

Think about people far away from you. How can you show them compassion?

humility

Humility is one of the greatest of all qualities, but one that is very difficult to practice.

The Bible even warns about this problem in Romans 12:3: "Because of the privilege and authority God has given me, I give each of you this warning: Don't think you are better than you really are. Be honest in your evaluation of yourselves, measuring yourselves by the faith God has given us."

Read Philippians 2:4-12 and Luke 14:7-11.
How would you define humility?

What can you do to practice humility?

unity

Even though we are different in so many ways, God wants us to live with a spirit of unity. Unity among people who celebrate and affirm their differences is a very important idea for followers of Jesus because our Creator, who loves diversity, also craves unity and oneness among His disciples.

In John 17:20-21 Jesus said, "I am praying not only for these disciples but also for all who will ever believe in me through their message. I pray that they will all be one, just as you and I are one—as you are in me, Father, and I am in you. And may they be in us so that the world will believe you sent me."

Read Colossians 1:15-22.
Think about God's diverse creation and how He brought it all together, including us, through Jesus. What does this mean to you personally?

The impact of our unity together can actually help convince people around us that God our Father did send His Son into the world. How can you help develop unity among the different Jesus-followers you know?

servant leadership

Jesus came *not* as a mighty king to sit upon a throne, but to serve and do something about the needs of others. Although He deserved a crown, He accepted the life of an ordinary man. He was a leader by serving others—not by commanding attention and using military might.

Read Matthew 20:25-28.
Put this into your own words. What does it mean to you?

What leaders do you know who are an example of this kind of leadership?

How can you be this kind of leader? What would need to change in your life?

prayer

Prayer formed the foundation of Jesus' life and ministry. Even on the cross, Jesus prayed. This regular conversation with God is one of the simplest, and yet most effective, ways that we can live like Jesus.

Read Luke 18:1-8 and Hebrews 5:7.
What can we learn from the parable of the woman in Luke 18:1-8?

What else can we learn from Jesus about prayer?

DO THIS AT HOME THIS WEEK

- Read "Loving Like Jesus" beginning on page 111 of this book.
- Use the guide here to create an action plan that will help you demonstrate the love of God to others in a variety of ways.

Loving Eyes

Looking at the man, Jesus felt genuine love for him. (Mark 10:21)

- Try to see your friends who don't follow Jesus the way our Father does.
- Observe their needs and try to help with those needs.
- Look for ways to be a friend.

Who can I look at with loving eyes this week?

Listening Ears

I wait quietly before God, for my victory comes from him. (Psalm 62:1)

- Stop what you're doing and be still.
- Pay attention when a friend is speaking. Let your friend speak without interrupting him or her.
- Maintain your interest and eye contact.

Who needs me to listen to them this week?

Serving Hands

So he got up from the table, took off his robe, wrapped a towel around his waist, and poured water into a basin. Then he began to wash the disciples' feet, drying them with the towel he had around him. (John 13:4-5)

- Let your actions be consistent with your words.
- Serve others by helping with their work or projects.
- Write a note of encouragement.

Who can I serve this week?

Prayerful Knees

One day Jesus told his disciples a story to show that they should always pray and never give up. (Luke 18:1)

Pray that:

- Circumstances in your friends' lives would open their eyes to their need for Jesus.
- God would make you sensitive to see opportunities to show them the love of Jesus Christ.
- Opportunities to share your stories together and share God's story in your life would happen.
- God's Spirit would convict them of their need for Him and a desire to repent and follow Jesus.

Who will I be on my knees praying for this week?

Encouraging Mouth

Instead, you must worship Christ as Lord of your life. And if someone asks about your Christian hope, always be ready to explain it. (1 Peter 3:15)

Worry weighs a person down; an encouraging word cheers a person up. (Proverbs 12:25)

- Call, write, or e-mail someone with words of encouragement.

Who needs encouragement from me this week?

Faith Journey

Willing Feet

> How beautiful on the mountains are the feet of the messenger who brings good news, the good news of peace and salvation, the news that the God of Israel reigns! (Isaiah 52:7)

Who can I go to this week to share the love of Jesus?

PRAYER TIME

Ask the Lord to help you understand what it means to live like Jesus — and then do it!

MEMORY VERSE

> In the same way, let your good deeds shine out for all to see, so that everyone will praise your heavenly Father. (Matthew 5:16)

Plan for Daily Growth

>> Let the message about Christ, in all its richness, fill your lives. Teach and counsel each other with all the wisdom he gives. Sing psalms and hymns and spiritual songs to God with thankful hearts. (Colossians 3:16)

a daily plan

Growing closer to Jesus is a daily process. It's not something we do once and then it's over. It's not even just going to church once a week. The way we get to know Jesus is by spending time with Him on a daily basis. Many people call their daily time with God "quiet time." Generally quiet time involves reading the Bible, praying, and being quiet and listening to God. Some people also include times of singing praise to God, and others write in a journal. There is no one way to have a quiet time, just as there isn't only one way that you'd spend time with a friend each day. It's okay to have variety in your time with God. Here are some important elements you'll want to include though.

quiet time

Quiet time is a specific and personal meeting with God where you talk to Him and He speaks to you. You might also call this your daily devotion time, your personal time with God, or anything else that reminds you to take time on a regular basis to be with God.

It's a time of seeking direction from Jesus. It can be a time of praise and prayer, study, thanksgiving, renewal, and growth.

Read John 15:1-11. When a branch is cut from a tree, it soon begins to wither and die because of lack of nutrition. The same happens when followers of Jesus cut themselves off from Him. It's important that we set time aside to be alone with God. That's where we'll find nourishment or food in our relationship with Him. The less time we spend listening to Him, the less spiritual nourishment we'll have to sustain us.

How would you express this passage in your own words?

What do you think it means to "remain" in Jesus?

requirements for quiet time

Be sure you have a Bible and an open, teachable spirit. It's also helpful to have a notebook or journal to write your thoughts, questions, and what you're learning (so you'll need a pen or pencil too!). Many people find it best to set aside the same time each day, such as first thing in the morning or during a quiet break in the day.

Can you think of any other reasons why having quiet time is important for your relationship with Jesus?

a sample quiet time

If you're new to this idea, you might want a few suggestions on what to do during a quiet time or daily devotion time. Here's an example of what you might do during this time:

1. Read a section of the Bible. This could be a whole chapter or just a few verses. Read it slowly, taking time to allow God to use these words to speak to you.
2. Talk to Jesus and ask Him to show you what He wants you to learn. We'll learn more about how to pray in quiet times later in this session.
3. Focus on a small section or verse or even a phrase of the passage you are reading that seems to have special meaning or relevance for you at that time. Read and re-read that small section over and over slowly, humbly before the Lord.
4. You may want to turn that piece of Scripture into a prayer. Talk to God, using the Bible as a guide for your conversation with Him.

Remember that the Lord's biggest desire is to connect with you. He is there when you seek Him out!

You'll find a few quiet times planned for you beginning on page 113 of this book. This section, "Quiet Time Guide," will walk you through a few quiet time sessions to help you get an idea of what these are like.

prayer

Devote yourselves to prayer with an alert mind and a thankful heart. (Colossians 4:2)

An essential part of quiet times is talking with God. We've said that prayer is simply talking to God, much like you'd talk to a friend. But what if you're not sure what to say? Here are some guidelines for how you can talk to God during your quiet times or anytime you want to pray. And notice that the first letters of each word spell "PRAY," which will make it easy for you to remember these guidelines.

Praise

> Enter his gates with thanksgiving; go into his courts with praise. Give thanks to him and praise his name. (Psalm 100:4)

> Everyone will share the story of your wonderful goodness; they will sing with joy about your righteousness. (Psalm 145:7)

God is so awesome that He deserves our highest honor. When we worship and praise God, our focus changes from ourselves to being completely focused on Him and His excellence. Praise moves us into God's presence.

When we praise God we tell Him how wonderful He is and what we love about Him. It might sound like this:

> Almighty God, you're worthy of my highest praise. I join all creation in giving glory to your majesty. Only you are worthy to receive all glory and praise.

Repent

> But if we confess our sins to him, he is faithful and just to forgive us our sins and to cleanse us from all wickedness. (1 John 1:9)

Repent means to have a change of mind and to turn and go the other way. It means we want to tell God what we've done wrong, say we're sorry, and then agree to stop doing those wrong actions.

Every one of us has failed and sinned. Yet God is always willing to forgive our sins and make us clean from every wrong when we confess our failures to Him. Then, with the help of the Holy Spirit, we can resolve with all our hearts to turn away from our faithlessness forever.

This part of your prayer time might sound like this:

> Lord, I have fallen short of your standards for me by (fill in the blank). Thank you that when I confess my failure you're faithful and just and will forgive me. Thank you for your mercy, and I receive your forgiveness. Please give me strength to say no when I am tempted again, and show me the way out.

Ask

Next comes the time to ask God for our needs, as well as the needs of others. We have moved into God's presence with praise and worship, and have removed all obstacles between us and Him through our confession and repentance. Now we can present our needs to Him, as well as the needs of others. His Word promises that He will not only listen, but He will also answer!

This part of your prayer may sound like this:

Heavenly Father, I know that you'll answer me when I call you. I present my needs to you. (And then tell Him what your needs are.) I know that nothing is too big or too hard for you. Please give me a heart of faith and a spirit that waits on you. Thank you for being my provider, my hope, and my help.

Yield

Yield means to give up our rights and our desires in favor of another person's rights or desires. Yielding to God becomes easier as we see God working mightily on our behalf. You'll become convinced of His great love and care for you, and that He will always do what is best for you. When you pray, trust God that His answer and His timing will be perfect for every situation you face. As you continue to surrender yourself to Him, God will work in you as well as through you.

This part of your prayer might sound like this:

Loving God, I give myself wholly to you. Be the Lord of my life. Rule and reign within my heart. Help me to have total trust and confidence in you, knowing that you have my best interest at heart. Please teach me to pray for what you know I need, not for what I want. Thank you for caring so much for me. I am ready to follow wherever you lead.

reading the bible

All Scripture is inspired by God and is useful to teach us what is true and to make us realize what is wrong in our lives. It corrects us when we are wrong and teaches us to do what is right. God uses it to prepare and equip his people to do every good work. (2 Timothy 3:16-17)

The Bible—the Word of God, or Scripture—is vital to a follower of Jesus. By spending time reading the Bible in your daily quiet time, you'll begin to gain a greater understanding of God and how He works.

Here are a few simple truths about the Bible:

The more we hear it, the more we'll recognize it.

Most of us have opportunities to *hear* the Word of God spoken—in church, during Bible studies, in school or Sunday school. We need to learn to hear Scripture when it is spoken. A way to develop this type of hearing is to take notes and later compare them with others who have also heard the lesson.

The more we read it, the more we'll learn.

Reading the Bible needs to be a daily activity. If possible, set up a plan to read the entire Bible over the course of one or two years. This continued exposure to Scripture will reveal to you the Bible in its entirety, rather than just the familiar stories and lessons.

The more we study it, the more we'll understand.

Studying the Bible is an opportunity for us to spend time with Jesus in His Word. Here are a few tips for Bible study:

1. It's good to read from both the Old and the New Testaments and particularly good to read and re-read the four Gospels at the beginning of the New Testament.
2. Be consistent. It's good to develop a habit or pattern for our quiet time with Jesus and follow a plan we've made.
3. Ask, *Does the passage say anything I don't understand?* Write down any questions you have about the passage to ask your leader or pastor later.
4. After reading a passage, think about what happened. Then write down what you think is the meaning or important lessons from this passage.

5. Decide how this passage could help you to be a better follower of Jesus. Decide how you can apply what you've learned to your own life. Applying what we learn so that others can experience the grace and kindness of Jesus through us is the whole point of growing like Jesus.

The more we memorize it, the more we can recall it when we need to.

The Lord will use the passages we memorize to comfort and direct us in our walk with Him. As you memorize verses, be sure to keep reviewing them and using them as much as possible. This will help you remember, instead of learning them one day and forgetting them the next.

The more we meditate upon it, the better established it will become in our minds.

Meditate and concentrate on the passage. This is not meditation about *emptying* our minds, but rather *filling* our minds with God's Word. The more we meditate on something, the more likely we're to learn and look at it from different perspectives. This helps to reinforce it in our memories and gives us a better idea of how we can apply it.

DO THIS AT HOME THIS WEEK

- Develop and write out a Bible study plan for the next month. Place a copy of this plan in your Bible. Ask a friend to follow the same plan so that you can hold each other accountable.
- Write a prayer to the Lord in your notebook. Incorporate the four points of P.R.A.Y.

Praise

Repent

Faith Journey

Ask

Yield

MEMORY VERSE

Trust in the Lord with all your heart; do not depend on your own understanding. Seek his will in all you do, and he will show you which path to take. (Proverbs 3:5-6)

Bonus!

In this section you'll find additional readings, as well as helpful tools for leading a small group using this book.

Becoming a Loving Parent

In most places around the world, being a parent is a very important thing. It confers great responsibilities, challenges, and privileges too. The father and mother are the head of the family, and their word carries a lot of weight. In many societies, the word of the eldest father, such as the grandfather or great-grandfather, is the law of the whole extended family. But not every man or woman is a responsible parent. There are certain qualifications young men and women must meet before they can become responsible parents. Some of these are:

maturity

A man or woman should be mature physically, emotionally, and mentally before becoming a parent.

What do you think it means to be mature physically? Emotionally? Mentally?

How does being mature in these ways help someone be a good parent?

having biological children

In some cultures a man's status soars in society when he has fathered a child, as does a woman's in other cultures when she bears a child.

Can someone be a good parent figure even if he or she has never had children? Explain your answer.

care, provision, and protection for the family

A parent has the responsibility of caring for his or her family, providing for their needs, and protecting them from danger. It is not enough to simply have children physically; they must be able to parent in these other ways also.

What happens when someone has children but can't care for them or protect them? Is this a good parent? Why or why not?

Around the world today there are many parents who, for different reasons, fail in their roles as fathers and mothers. As a result, the family and small local communities are struggling to survive as healthy places to raise children. Over time the values that bind our society together are being eroded, and some communities are experiencing one crisis after the other. It is time for parents to rise up to bring healing, care, provision, and protection for our families.

As we go through the studies of God our Father, may we learn and embrace the qualities of God, the perfect parent, so that we can grow to be godly parents ourselves.

How do you think knowing more about God, the perfect Father, can help you to become a better parent, either now or in the future?

God the Father – A True Story

I grew up in a single-parent family. My father was never introduced to me, so I don't know what it really means to have a father at home. When I became a follower of Jesus and I asked Him to come into my life, to direct and take charge of me forever, the idea of God being my Father was introduced to me. It only remained as a good idea in my mind, however, and I could never really relate to it. The main reason for this was that I never had a mental picture of what a father would be like. It's just like telling somebody about a car when he or she has never seen one. It has been so difficult for me to truly relate with God as Father, though this never changed the fact that God is really my heavenly Father.

As I continue to read the Bible and pray to Jesus, the understanding of God being my heavenly Father is becoming more real day after day. The prayer I have begun to pray lately is, "Dear God, please help me to understand you more as Father."

> Jesus replied, "I tell you the truth, unless you are born again, you cannot see the Kingdom of God." (John 3:3)

I do believe Jesus meant being spiritually born and becoming part of the family of God. This truth of being born from above and becoming part of

God's family makes the idea of God being my heavenly Father much more clear.

Another Scripture that helps me to understand my heavenly Father is Romans 8:14-16:

> For all who are led by the Spirit of God are children of God. So you have not received a spirit that makes you fearful slaves. Instead, you received God's Spirit when he adopted you as his own children. Now we call him, "Abba, Father." For his Spirit joins with our spirit to affirm that we are God's children.

God has continued to show me that He is my heavenly Father and that I am His child.

— George

I Am Your Father

My child, don't judge me by your human experience of a father. Your natural father was a man who failed in many ways. You were aware of his weaknesses, as well as his strengths.

Some people have suffered rejection at the hands of their human fathers because they were men who could not be trusted. They were unjust or unconcerned about their children. I never abuse my children. I am near to all who call on me. I am never distant. I comfort, strengthen, and heal them. So I am not to be compared with any other father.

I am not a man. There are no weak, vulnerable areas in my life. There is never inadequacy in me or inability to meet a need. I love you with my everlasting love; it will never be withdrawn from you. As your Father, I watch over your development, and I am concerned to protect you from things that are dangerous and harmful to you.

You haven't always heeded my warnings, so at times you've been hurt. But I have always been on hand to heal you and meet your need. Sometimes you've allowed me to do this; at other times you haven't.

I never deal with you as you deserve, but only with compassion and grace. This is difficult for you to understand. I give and give and go on giving to you. I never come to the end of my giving.

You often think to yourself, *Who am I that I should receive such love, that I should know the personal affection of my God?* You fear that my love might be withdrawn suddenly and then you'll feel rejected. If you were to open yourself fully to me and then I turned away, you would be devastated. But I would never treat you like that.

I don't withdraw my love. I don't commit myself to you only for a set period of time. My commitment to you is unending, as a commitment of love must always be. Love cannot be real if it is ever withdrawn.

I already know you, every part of you—and yet I love you. I see what you try to hide from me. Hiding is futile. I'll not stop loving you just because I uncover some unsavory part of your character. My love for you is real. It doesn't depend on who you are, but on who I am![1]

---

1. Colin Urquhart, *My Dear Child: Listening to God's Heart* (Lake Mary, FL: Creation House, 1991), 28-29. Used with permission.

The Son

the promise in the old testament

The Bible contains both the Old and the New Testaments. The Old Testament is an account of God's relationship with the Hebrew people (the Israelites) and teaches the history, laws, and way of life for the people of Israel.

As part of their relationship with God, the Israelites followed the Law, religious traditions, and commands set out by God. Sacrifices and prayers, feasts, and fasts were ways the Israelites and others wishing to follow God kept their commitment and relationship with Him.

God only meant the Law to be a temporary means of bringing people into a relationship with Him. He knew humanity would fail to keep the Law, so God made a promise to humans. God the Father promised that He would send a Savior to be the final and perfect sacrifice — the sacrifice that would save humanity forever, enabling intimate relationship between God and people once again.

The Old Testament is an account of how God prepares the way for the coming of His Son as this Savior. In many parts it speaks about the future coming of the Messiah, His birth, life, work, and even His sacrificial death. These promises were fulfilled with the birth of our Savior, Jesus Christ, in Bethlehem to a virgin named Mary.

the coming in the new testament

The New Testament is the account of this coming of Jesus into the world, and it gives meaning and explanation to the remarkable prophesies made in the Old Testament. The world has been changed forever because of this amazing event. Jesus is the anointed one, the long-awaited Messiah, the Christ, and Son of God. In Him, God became a man, entering our world to provide the way for all people to know Him and have an opportunity for a personal relationship with Him.

He wants us to know that He loves us so much that He was willing to leave His perfect home in heaven to come to earth where He was beaten, cursed, ridiculed, ignored, and killed. He understands what we experience in life because He experienced it too. He did this because He loves us. He gave Himself to be the only perfect sacrifice that could be made to save us from the faithlessness and rebellion that leads to death and eternal separation from God.

What does this mean to you?

Understanding Salvation

As a growing disciple of Jesus, there are three aspects of our salvation that are important to understand.

1. we are justified

This means we have been redeemed and rescued, and the penalty for our sins has been paid.

Note that this is in the *past tense*—we *have been* delivered from the penalty of our sins.

At the moment Christ died on the cross our rebellion was paid for, and when we turned to Jesus, seeking forgiveness for our thoughts, actions, and attitudes, we were made clean and right through the saving grace of Jesus Christ. We joined God's family.

> But God showed his great love for us by sending Christ to die for us while we were still sinners. And since we have been made right in God's sight by the blood of Christ, he will certainly save us from God's condemnation (Romans 5:8-9)

2. we are sanctified

This means we are made holy, separate, and unpolluted.

Note that this is in the *present tense*—we *are being* renewed through the grace of the Holy Spirit within us.

By faith, we're daily surrendering our lives and trusting God to make us holy and more like Christ. Our character and conduct are constantly being refined and changed by the Holy Spirit in us.

> But now you are free from the power of sin and have become slaves of God. Now you do those things that lead to holiness and result in eternal life. (Romans 6:22)

3. we will be glorified

This means we will be exalted, elevated, lifted up by God.

Note that this is the *future tense*—we *will* live in the presence of God eternally.

Because we're in a right relationship with God through what Jesus has done, the Lord has promised us the gift of life with Him forever.

> For his Spirit joins with our spirit to affirm that we are God's children. And since we are his children, we are his heirs. In fact, together with Christ we are heirs of God's glory. But if we are to share his glory, we must also share his suffering. Yet what we suffer now is nothing compared to the glory he will reveal to us later. (Romans 8:16-18)

Loving Like Jesus

Jesus tells us to love others as He loves us, but how do we do that? Jesus literally gave His life for us. Is that what Jesus wants us to do? How can we love like Jesus? What does that mean?

This section will help us look more closely at what it means to love like Jesus and how we can do that.

God loves us — we can love others

Read Ephesians 2:1-10.

God lavishly gives His love and gifts to us, His children. This gives Him great pleasure, and as we do the same to others we, too, experience our Father's pleasure.

Ephesians 2:10 says, "For we are God's masterpiece. He has created us anew in Christ Jesus, so we can do the good things he planned for us long ago." We were created to do good things!

But notice that God didn't wait around for us to become good before He loved us. He loved us when we were filled with sin. This means that we have the ability to love others even when they're not easy to love.

love brings community and oneness

God's love is not only for a select few. God is amazingly inclusive and through Jesus has shown us how we can achieve unity and oneness with those around us. It can be achieved by being gracious and loving, giving out of His love and generosity to us. Sharing His love and compassion to *everyone*, regardless of their sex, race, color, or status, fulfills the promise that Jesus is "good news that will bring great joy to all people" (Luke 2:10).

it's about love, not duty

> This is my commandment: Love each other in the same way I have loved you. There is no greater love than to lay down one's life for one's friends. (John 15:12-13)

Even though Jesus says love is a commandment, it's actually God's gift for humanity. He loves us and wants us to enjoy Him. We'll enjoy our life far more when we live out of His grace and give it away to others. Jesus says that when we feed the hungry, provide shelter and drink, give clothing and care to the injured—when we do this to the least, the small, the lost, and the lonely of the world—we're doing it to Him (Matthew 25:34-40).

What changes in my life would help me love others more like Jesus?

Who are the people around me I can show love to with my words and actions this week?

Quiet Time Guide

Try using these quiet time guides over the next few days to help you get more comfortable having a time of personal devotions. Each one is a little different from the others to let you see the variety you might have in your time with God.

Psalm 37

- Read the passage through slowly.
- Come to Jesus and open your heart to Him.
- Read a small section that stands out to you over and over, slowly drinking it in.
- Turn the words into a prayer and pray in a calm and gentle manner.
- Remember, take your time and allow yourself to go with the Spirit, and write down what comes to your mind and your heart in your journal.
- Write down questions you have about this passage or your faith, or portions of this passage that are especially meaningful to you.
- Note any actions that you'll take this week to apply what you've learned.
- Write any specific prayers you have for the day, as well as answers to prayer.

Philippians 4:8-9

- What is the key message of this passage?
- Write this passage in your own words.
- Ask God to show you what He wants you to learn through this passage.
- Is there something you do not understand? Write it down to ask someone later.
- How can you apply this passage to your life today?
- What difference will it make in your life if you do what this passage says?

Joshua 1:5-9

- What is the key message of this passage?
- Write this passage in your own words.
- Read a small section that stands out to you over and over, slowly drinking it in.
- Write down questions you have about this passage or your faith, or portions of this passage that are especially meaningful to you.
- Note any actions that you'll take this week to apply what you've learned.
- Write any specific prayers you have for the day, as well as answers to prayer.

Psalm 19:7-8

- Ask God to help you see His plan for you through His Word.
- What is the key message of this passage?
- Write this passage in your own words.
- Is there something you do not understand? Write it down to ask someone later.
- How can you apply this passage to your life today?
- What difference will it make in your life if you do what this passage says?

2 Timothy 3:14-4:5

- Read the passage through slowly.
- Come to Jesus and open your heart to Him.
- Read a small section that stands out to you over and over, slowly drinking it in.
- Remember, take your time and allow yourself to go with the Spirit, and write down what comes to your mind and your heart in your journal.
- Write down questions you have about this passage or your faith, or portions of this passage that are especially meaningful to you.
- Write any specific prayers you have for the day, as well as answers to prayer.

Small Group Leader's Guide

How to Lead a Small Group

If you're using this book with a small group, you'll find it's easy to follow along. Simply read sections in each session aloud together, and when you're instructed to write your reflections, take additional time to discuss these in your group instead of just writing those thoughts.

You'll also find additional ideas for each session later in this section. These are optional ideas, but they'll help get your group thinking about the topic at hand. Give them a try!

Here are a few more tips that will make your group a success.

- Be sure your small groups really are small. If you have more than six people in your group, form smaller groups. By keeping groups at six or fewer members, you allow everyone time to talk, and people will generally open up and be more honest when sharing in a very small group.
- Take your time and work through each session, allowing time for Scripture reading, discussion, and prayer. Allow at least an hour for each session. You may want to allow more time so no one feels rushed during discussion.
- When there are lists of passages to look up and comment on, assign different small groups the different passages. Allow them several

minutes to look up and read their passage, and discuss it together. Then have each group report back to the larger group about what they read, what they learned, and what their action steps might be.

- Ask each person to also do the "Do This at Home This Week" section during the week before you meet again. It's a great idea to have at least ten minutes at the beginning of each meeting to hear reports back on how people did with these challenges. Celebrate the growth you see in each other's lives as you hear what's happened since you last met.
- Don't let any one person monopolize the discussions. Encourage everyone to share, and monitor the discussion by drawing out the quieter people with questions such as, "We haven't heard from Mali yet—let us hear your opinion, Mali." Or "We've heard a lot from Rasheen on this question, but I want to be sure everyone has a chance to share. Tony, what are your thoughts?" Be gentle, but do let it be known that everyone is equal in the discussion.
- Remind group members that what's shared at group is confidential. No one wants to be the subject of gossip.
- Everyone in your group will need a Bible and pen, along with a copy of this book. Encourage responsibility by asking everyone to remember to bring these.
- Start on time and end on time. It honors the commitment of those who are attending.
- Provide snacks. Okay, this is optional, but you'll find everyone will appreciate it!

Group Discussion Starters

In this section you'll find optional activities to use with your small group. These can be used to begin each of your sessions as a way to engage your group and prepare them for further reflection and discussion.

SESSION ONE: ENTERING A RELATIONSHIP WITH GOD
This is a good way to introduce the topic of a new relationship.
Have everyone answer this question:

Tell about a friendship you still have today that got off to a good start right from the very beginning. What was different about that friendship?

After everyone shares, comment on things that were similar in each person's story. How can we use what we know from our friendships to get off to a good start in our relationship with God?

SESSION TWO: WHO IS GOD?
The topic of the Trinity can be difficult to grasp. This helps everyone think about other things they accept but may not understand. You'll need paper and pencils.
Ask everyone to form groups of three or four. Have each group list as

many things that they don't understand as possible. For example, gravity, the size of the universe, a new mathematic concept recently learned in class, and so on. See how many each group can list in just two or three minutes.

Have each group read their list. Ask group members to consider this: Do they believe these concepts are true even though they're hard to understand? Why or why not?

How do we come to the point of believing something is true, even if we don't understand it?

SESSION THREE: GOD THE FATHER
This activity helps everyone realize that the perfect father doesn't exist on earth—leading into your session on God as the perfect heavenly Father. You'll need paper and pencils.

Have everyone get into small groups of three or four. Tell the groups they need to create the perfect father, drawing qualities or talents from famous people they know of. For example, they might have a father with the strength of a popular athlete, the intelligence of Albert Einstein, the looks of a famous actor, and so on.

After groups have invented their perfect father, have them share their results. Comment on how impossible it is to really have the perfect father here on earth as you lead into your session on God, the perfect heavenly Father.

SESSION FOUR: THE FATHER AND YOU
This helps everyone think about what a loving father does to show that love.

Have everyone share his or her answer to this question:

> What would be the perfect outing or perfect day that you would wish for with your dad?

If anyone doesn't have a father for any reason, let that person describe what the perfect outing or day would be like with an imaginary father.

After everyone has described how a father would treat him or her on this day, move into your session on how God views us. You might want to end your session by thinking about a perfect day with God!

SESSION FIVE: THE SON OF GOD

This icebreaker helps everyone think about sacrifices they've made, which pale in comparison to the sacrifice Jesus made for us. You'll need paper, pencils, and a basket or other container.

Give each person a piece of paper and pencil. Explain that each person should write about a sacrifice he or she made for someone else, without writing a name on the paper. For example, someone might write, "I gave up the biggest piece of cake so my sister could have it," or another might write, "I worked extra hours for a month to save enough money to buy my girlfriend a necklace for her birthday."

When everyone has written about a sacrifice, have them fold the papers and collect them in the basket or other container. Mix the papers and redistribute them. Have everyone take turns reading the papers aloud, and try to guess who wrote each one.

Comment on the variety of sacrifices made as you begin your session on the ultimate sacrifice.

SESSION SIX: JESUS AS MAN AND SAVIOR

This is a simple question, but it helps everyone think about the reality of Jesus' humanity.

Have everyone share his or her answer to this question:

What do you think Jesus was like when He was your age?

Encourage everyone to consider that Jesus once *was* their age. What might He have been like? Would they have been friends?

SESSION SEVEN: GOD THE HOLY SPIRIT

The idea of a helper we cannot see can be confusing for some people. This discussion helps everyone remember there are other things in the world that we rely on but cannot see.

See how many things your group can list that are invisible but real and powerful. You might share one or two ideas to get everyone started, but let the group see how many they can think of. Some they might name are:

- wind
- gravity

- electricity
- radio waves
- sound waves

Ask about the different ways these (and the others they name) are used, and what power they have. How can something invisible to us have power? Does understanding things in our physical world that are unseen but powerful help them understand the Holy Spirit? Why or why not?

SESSION EIGHT: THE HOLY SPIRIT AND US

One aspect of this session is the ability of the Holy Spirit to comfort us. Use this opening time of prayer to turn to the Holy Spirit for that comfort.

Have everyone form smaller groups of three or four. Explain that you'd like group members to share about a place in their lives where they need comfort right now. This might be comfort over illness, the need of a job, stress with classes, or any other reason that a person is feeling the need for comfort.

Then take time for the smaller groups to pray together, asking God to provide that comfort through the Holy Spirit.

SESSION NINE: THE FATHER, SON, AND HOLY SPIRIT

This discussion helps group members wrestle with questions they still have about the Trinity.

Explain that you're going to give a few examples of things that are "three in one." Group members should then give their thoughts on how your example is like the Trinity, as well as how it is unlike the Trinity.

- Water, steam, ice
- Egg (shell, yolk, white)
- A man who is a father, brother, and son

See what areas everyone agrees are like the Trinity, and what examples are not as good in helping to understand this concept.

SESSION TEN: JESUS AS LORD

This activity helps group members consider the concept of having a lord in their lives.

Ask: What would it take for you to bow down to someone?

In some parts of the world, people bow as a greeting or to show respect. In other parts of the world, people don't bow for any reason—it's simply not done. So what would it take for you to bow down to someone? Would that person need to be powerful? Rich? Kind? Or would you bow to someone easily?

Use this discussion to get everyone thinking about the concept of a lord. What does it mean to bow to someone else and let them be your ruler?

SESSION ELEVEN: LIVING LIKE JESUS

Get everyone moving with a silly game of Follow the Leader to get them thinking about following the lead of Jesus.

Begin by having everyone line up, and then start a game of Follow the Leader. Make it challenging by skipping, hopping on one foot, running, or doing unusual combinations of steps. Take turns and let other group members be the leader too.

When everyone is tired and laughing, return to your seats and talk about people everyone would like to follow. Who are people whose actions you'd be glad to follow, no matter how hard?

Use this to lead into your session on living like Jesus and following His perfect example.

SESSION TWELVE: PLAN FOR DAILY GROWTH

Our spiritual growth is similar to the growth of a plant. Bring in any plant—a houseplant, a planted flower—or go outside and stand around a bush or tree.

Have everyone look at the plant and name the things it needs for growth. Surely they'll think of sunshine, nutrients, soil, water, and time. How do these compare to what we need to grow spiritually? See if group members can think of an analogy for each thing the plant needs that compares to each thing we need. For example, sunshine might represent time in prayer, and soil might represent a heart open to the words of God. Encourage your group to be creative!

Youth for Christ

Youth for Christ is a global indigenous Christian youth movement active in one hundred nations worldwide.

YFC programs are led by a national director and board made up of nationals from each country. In this way, YFC is able to reach young people around the world in a context that makes sense to them and their culture.

YFC has successfully reached young people with the gospel of Christ since the 1940s. From its then first employee, Billy Graham, to the now 35,000 international staff and volunteers, YFC continues to minister to young people worldwide.

God is calling Youth for Christ to invest in reaching and engaging young people for Jesus Christ, equipping them as His disciples and empowering them as godly leaders to transform the world.

YFC's strategic focus is to reach young people everywhere, working together with the local church and other like-minded partners to raise up lifelong followers of Jesus who lead by their godliness in lifestyle, devotion to the Word of God and prayer, passion for sharing the love of Christ, and commitment to social involvement.

Also Available in the YOUTH FOR CHRIST JOURNEY Series!

Youth for Christ presents the JOURNEY series, a four-part Bible study that looks closely at the basic concepts of leadership, sharing your faith, God's kingdom, and spiritual warfare. In each study, you'll find an easy-to-read format with stories from around the world, Scripture, and lots of space to write down your thoughts.

Reaching Out
ISBN-13: 978-1-60006-313-8
ISBN-10: 1-60006-313-6

There's a long list of reasons you might not feel compelled to share your faith: fear, insecurity, lack of knowledge. There's just one powerful reason you should share it: love. This study helps you dig through Scripture to uncover the foundations and basic skills for sharing your faith and building God's kingdom.

Influencing Others
ISBN-13: 978-1-60006-315-2
ISBN-10: 1-60006-315-2

Leadership isn't just about power, authority, fame, or money; it's about influencing others and making things happen. Along with learning the characteristics of leaders and how to influence people in a godly way, you'll discover the importance of serving the ones who follow you and serving Christ as you lead.

Spiritual Warfare
ISBN-13: 978-1-60006-316-9
ISBN-10: 1-60006-316-0

Are you confused about spiritual warfare and what it involves? You're not alone. Lots of people are in the dark about battling the powers of darkness. Learn what spiritual warfare is and how praise, prayer, and authority are used. Battle the darkness with the power of God.

To order copies, call NavPress at
1-800-366-7788, or log on to www.navpress.com.